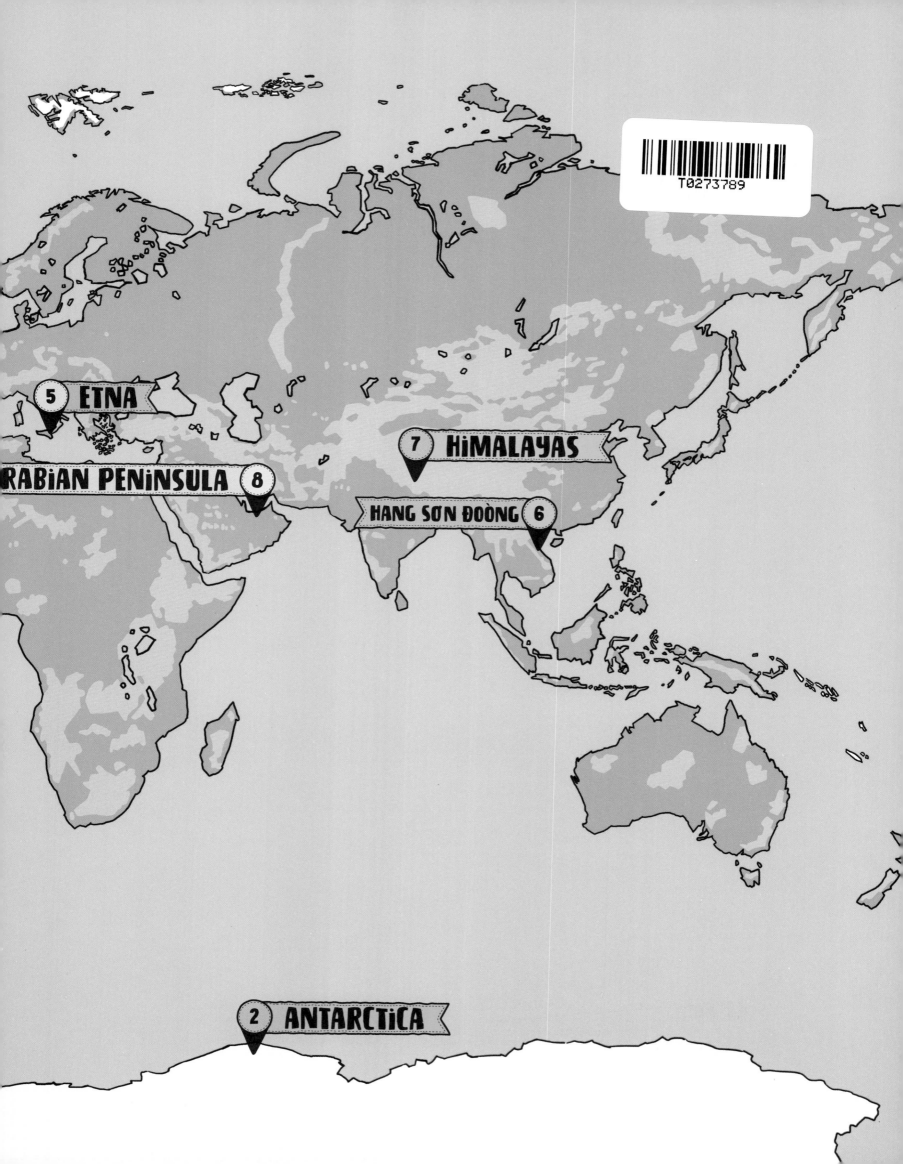

WORLD OF
EXTREME
ADVENTURES

To everyone who can see the world

as a big adventure

WORLD OF EXTREME ADVENTURES

Written by **Helena Haraštová**
Illustrated by **Lukáš Fibrich**

Albatros

WORLD OF EXTREME ADVENTURES

When we were little, we would imagine that we were pirates on a sailboat in a stormy sea ... adventurers wandering to the nearest oasis for all we were worth ... American Indians on the warpath—owowow! ... astronauts in a space shuttle heading toward new planets ...

And this desire for adventure continued even as we got older. Every weekend, we devoured TV shows about explorers who drove criss-cross globally, and we tried to shoot our own stories of the trips, the training, the expeditions into the unknown ...

Extreme places? Extreme experiences? Well, that'll be fun, haha!

As a born leader, I signed up to be the head of our expedition. I can talk to anyone, I never get lost and I'll make sure the lazy ones keep up the pace. Sound good?

If I can contribute to this expedition in any way, then I guess ... it's with knowledge. I love to read, and what I read, I remember. Actually, I'm a little scared ... But sit at home when my buddies go on an adventure? No way!

Well, the way I see it, this bunch needs someone smart and reasonable. And that's me!

YUNA

DANIEL

OLIVER

EMMA

And then it hit us: how about we shoot our own travel show? Overcoming real obstacles, discovering **THE EXTREMES** of our planet, proving children can also travel the world—and recording this very special journey on a camera, or just on a phone . . . We will do our best!

TRAVEL PREPARATIONS

Training: We train properly every day to have enough muscle, endurance, and fitness.

First-Aid Course: How do you treat a fracture? What do you do in case you get a fever? How do you recognize food poisoning? When do you see a doctor immediately? We already know everything perfectly!

Geography: The alpha and omega of our expedition. It's so important that we find out as much informa tion as possible about each destination and learn a few words of the local language in advance.

Documentary Preparation: We meet to decide why we want to shoot our show and what should and shouldn't be in it. We need to learn to work with equipment and make a detailed filming schedule.

WHAT WE TAKE WITH US

1. Waterproof boots
2. Thermo jacket
3. Sleeping mat
4. Sleeping bag
5. First-aid kit
6. Diary
7. Tripod
8. Reserve batteries
9. Polaroid
10. Notebook computer
11. Backpack
12. Snorkel
13. Charger
14. Outdoor bottle
15. Baseball cap

CANADA

Hellooo, can you see me? A huge forest fire brought us to the heart of the Canadian boreal forest. The rumbling you can hear is from our firefighting plane's engine. We are now 1400 feet above the burning forest, and just a minute ago, the smoke jumpers dove straight into the fiery hell. I'll try to zoom them in for you. They're packing their parachutes right now. Radiant heat is reaching us up here . . .

DAY 1: The **smoke jumpers** battled the destructive force of fire face to face. They put out fires in places where heavy machinery simply won't reach. We set out to lend a hand . . .

DAY 2: There was a **cross-country mountain bike** race nearby, and Yuna simply had to try. Wow! A terrain full of rocks, boulders, steep slopes, and exposed tree roots doesn't allow for any mistakes!

DAY 3: Kayaking among killer whales is nothing like diving with dolphins—'cause killer whales are bloodthirsty predators! Fortunately, we got out alive this time. Without a phone and soaked from top to toe.

DAY 4: In the extreme climate of the Canadian north, local Inuits wanted to treat us with their traditional delicacy—**muktuk**. Frozen pieces of whale skin with fat? Well, we'll stick with chocolate, thanks . . .

THE **COOLEST GUYS**

Would you like to become a smoke jumper? First, you can't be afraid of heights, fire, or the wilderness. Second, you need to be super fast. When the alarm goes off, you have only a few minutes to pack your equipment. Then, you jump straight off the plane, which will continue giving you information about the fire.

HOW TO SURVIVE **A FIRE** IN THE WILD

- Call the **emergency** number, and state your location.
- If there is a **waterbody**, go through it to the other side.
- Cover your **nose** and **mouth** with a wet cloth.
- Lie **face down** and cover yourself with a wet blanket
- If you don't have a blanket, **cover yourself** in mud or bury yourself in the dirt.

FOREST FIRES

"This dang fire was caused by lightning, that bastard!"

- Forest fires are **natural** and even **beneficial**.
- New vegetation grows and the landscape is **cleared**.
- Droughts and global warming = increase in forest fires + faster spread + proximity to populated areas.
- **Toxic and harmful** substances leak into the air during large-scale fires.

SMOKE JUMPERS
EQUIPMENT

- Heavy padded firefighter's suit
- Boots, axe, and helmet
- Food and drinks
- Headlamp
- Sleeping bag

CROSS-COUNTRY CYCLING
LETS YOU FLY

Practice this extreme sport on any challenging or uneven landscape. But whether you decide to conquer the pitfalls of nature in a forest, a mountain, or a desert or you prefer to that on man-made obstacles and springboards, never forget your helmet and protective gear. If you end up having a nasty fall, the pain won't be easy!

HOW TO **PHOTOGRAPH** EXTREME **SPORTS**

Speed and unpredictability are typical of extreme sports—the exact opposite of what a photographer needs! But don't worry. Try . . .

Close monitoring
Wide-angle lens will capture movement in its full width, but an action-packed photo will include only a cut-out of the athlete's figure.

Emotions
They are strong at the starting line!

Unusual points of view
Lie down on the grass, or look through a wooden fence.

KILLER WHALES, RUTHLESS KILLERS

A cute, slightly overgrown black-and-white dolphin? Think twice!

> The Latin name "orca" means **a sea monster**—a demon from the depths.

> The Haids, living near the coast of British Columbia, call it "skana"—**a killing demon**.

But you don't really have to be afraid of killer whales, as attacks on humans or ships are rare. On the other hand, sitting in a kayak and sailing directly into their group could be a provocation. Right, Daniel?
We recorded our encounter with a killer whale, but then, we somehow ... lost the record ...

A **DANGEROUS** INUIT **FEAST**

Inuits have a very peculiar cuisine.
They gave us another specialty—igunaq.

HOW TO **PREPARE IGUNAQ**:

1) Bury raw walrus meat: 2) wait one year until the meat ferments and freezes, and (3) finally, dig the meat out and hold a celebration!

While the locals are completely used to this diet, foreigners are in potential danger of botulism, poisoning caused by bacteria reproducing in the absence of air. Even a small dose is fatal!

We were lucky and survived!

Panning
Move your camera following the same direction and speed as the athlete. The result is a sharp shot with a blurred background.

Sequential shots and continuous focus
This trick will increase your chances of capturing a crucial moment.

Welcome to places few get to see. These plains are densely snow covered with a few strange-looking small buildings. That's Antarctica—the coldest continent. We took advantage of the three-month period when reaching here is even possible, and the international research team kindly invited us to the polar station. We have food, drink supplies, and all the equipment needed for the whole following year. Unbelievably, summer has just arrived. What awaits us now?

DAY 5: Local scientists **researched ancient layers of ice** to obtain information on the history of life on Earth. We used a special drill to obtain long ice poles.

DAY 8: The whole time we were wondering how come there were always fresh vegetables in the kitchen—in Antarctica where it's impossible to grow anything?! But then, we found a miracle right next to the main building: **a hydroponic greenhouse**!

ANTARCTiCA

DAY 6: After a long day outside, we felt like icicles, so we decided to stay at **the base**. The little bedrooms were modest, but there were a lot of activities to do: what about cinema or gym?

DAY 7: Brrr ... ddd-don't ttt--try this on your own! **A polar plunge** is for lovers of true extremes—you jump in ice-cold water wearing only your swimsuit. But where else can you experience something like this?

11

PROTECT YOUR DEVICES

- Store your camera in a waterproof bag. Pull it out only for a few moments. For this, first decide what you want to photograph.
- Avoid condensed humidity by using waterproof case.
- Changing the lens in freezing weather can be quite annoying. It's better to invest in more stand-alone cameras that you can rotate.
- Keep your batteries warm. They will last much longer.
- Keep the memory card protected from the cold.

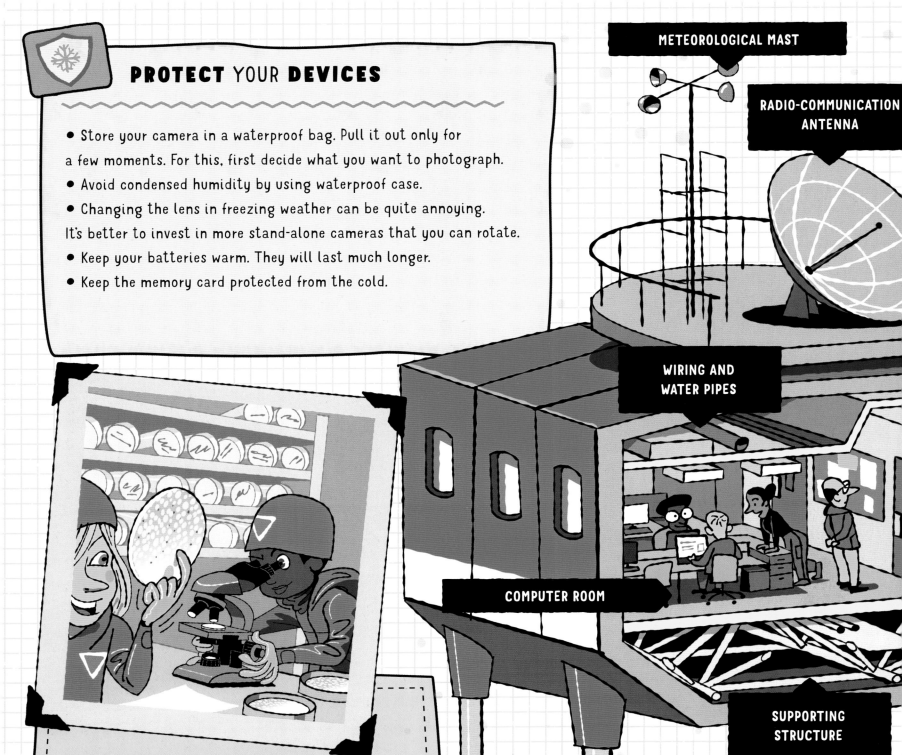

METEOROLOGICAL MAST

RADIO-COMMUNICATION ANTENNA

WIRING AND WATER PIPES

COMPUTER ROOM

SUPPORTING STRUCTURE

HYDRAULIC STEEL PROPS

SEARCHING FOR LIFE

Maybe it seems like unnecessarily expensive to drill into ice and examine long ice poles or their thin cuts. But in fact, these layers of varying ages tell us **a lot about the Earth's history**. In certain areas of Antarctica, several miles under the surface, ancient lakes lie hidden. Once trapped by layers of glacier, they haven't been touched by sunlight in millions of years! Bacteria that we don't find anywhere else on Earth could still live in such waters.

A HEARTY SNACK

The best local tradition: pack a bar of chocolate whenever you go for a walk! It lasts long and tastes good even in a blizzard, unlike the traditional pemmican—mixture of meat, fat, and fruit—which smells really bad!

WHAT TO DO IN A **BLIZZARD**

The weather in Antarctica changes by the minute. One day, we flew further inland to where we were supposed to do some research. But as soon as we lost sight of the plane, a storm arrived. The snow and piercing wind were so fierce that not only was our visibility cut off, but our mobility was also thwarted. We had to set up an emergency tent. This changed after several hours, as if by magic. Scary—brrrrr!

LABORATORY

LAYERED **LIKE AN ONION**

Although Yuna tried to test the very first day how long she could endure the cold outside only in her pajamas, she was back in the warmth of the base in a minute. When you're here, layer on!

① Long and quality thermal underwear
② Warm fleece layer
③ Waterproof layer
④ Woolen socks
⑤ Waterproof shoes
⑥ Waterproof cap

COMFY LIFE AT THE BASE

There are about 70 permanently accommodated polar stations in Antarctica. Scientists and maintenance workers from around the world take turns here. Everyone stays here only for a few months and are all so nice and friendly! Even when we disturb them in the lab, where they process the samples.

ATACAMA

I feel like we've landed on an alien planet. Before our lungs get used to the 8200-foot altitude, we'll have a little trouble breathing here. But don't worry, we'll get used to it. Just look around! A rocky wasteland, as if dinosaurs had been walking on it yesterday, and those endless red sand plains, like from a sci-fi movie! It hasn't rained here in many years. What is life like in the driest place on Earth? Let's discover it together!

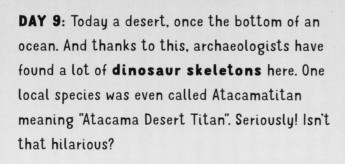

DAY 9: Today a desert, once the bottom of an ocean. And thanks to this, archaeologists have found a lot of **dinosaur skeletons** here. One local species was even called Atacamatitan meaning "Atacama Desert Titan". Seriously! Isn't that hilarious?

DAY 11: **Copper mines** bring a whole lotta wealth to the Atacama Desert, but they also make life uncomfortable. It's not just that—the air near the mine smells funny. It contains harmful and often toxic substances.

DAY 12: We could not miss out the opportunity to witness the famous local **motorcycle** rally. It takes place over several days, so we must sleep in the desert. Wish us luck! Ready, set, GO!

DAY 10: The giant telescopes of local **astronomical observatories** can look far into space and explore its various corners. Emma, do you want to add something? What?! Where?! Shoot it, Oliver!

EXPLORING THE UNIVERSE

In the Atacama Desert, we sometimes feel like we're on Mars. The truth is NASA tests machines designed to explore the Red Planet here. Also, its dry air, high altitude, clear sky, and zero light pollution make it the perfect place for space observation. Using devices, scientists from across the world can see how stars and planets formed a long time ago.

WHY ISN'T THERE ANY RAIN IN THE ATACAMA DESERT?

Although there is a little rain here from time to time, some places in the desert have not seen rain for about 400 years. High atmospheric pressure in this region brings **dry air** to the ground, and at the same time, the desert is located in the **rain shadow** of the nearby Andes—the rain clouds from the east run out of water on the opposite side of the mountains.

SQUEALING DELICACY

Luck has always been on our side when our tummies grumble. A few Indians were roasting something temptingly aromatic over a fire at a distance—we went closer and found roasted wild guinea pigs turning over the flames. Yum! Or was it?

TREACHEROUS NIGHTS

You already know that we took part in a motorcycle rally across the Atacama Desert, but what you don't know is that we got Daniel to race just by promising to spend the night in the desert and enjoy the clear starry sky. And we were lucky: the sky showed us not only the constellations but also the Milky Way! The air temperature, however, was far from nice during the day, and at night, we were shivering with cold. It was only 41 degree Fahrenheit!

NIGHT

temperature

41 °F

DREADED SCORPIONS

This tiny creature can cause many inconveniences. Being solely at fault, we decided to spend the night in its hunting ground. If Emma didn't have her eyes wide open, we would probably be solving completely different problems instead of filming a documentary. Daniel later found out from his cell phone in his tent that the red scorpion, originally from Mexico, is one of the most poisonous creatures ever. Shocking! Its poison damages nerves and muscles and even causes breathing problems and cardiac arrest.

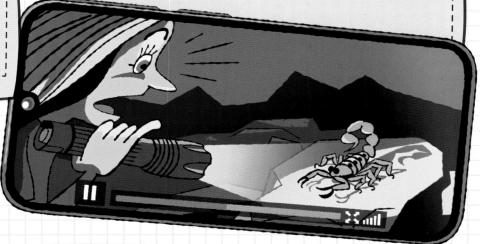

EASY NIGHT SKY PHOTOS

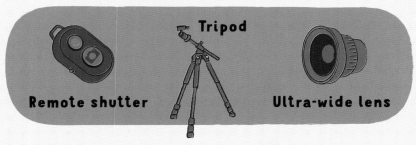

Remote shutter **Tripod** **Ultra-wide lens**

- Capture something from the Earth too, such as a forest or a rock. The contrast is worth it.
- You can achieve better visibility with wide-open apertures.
- Focus manually.
- Take a picture of the movement of the stars! When you take a photo of the night sky with a tripod and a remote shutter, the result will be an impressive capture of stellar orbits.
- Photograph the moon during a full moon. For the stars though, wait until a new moon.

We are so happy to show you this expedition. We managed to negotiate a rare permit to enter a strictly forbidden area, and you bet you will never be allowed to visit this place. The Brazilian island of Ilha da Queimada Grande, also known as Snake Island, is inhabited by the highly venomous Bothrops insularis, commonly known as the Golden Lancehead. This was a very dangerous trip . . .

DAY 13: We do not even have to look for them—just stop and listen. Hiss . . . hiss . . . hiss . . . **Snakes are everywhere!** We count one to five of them at each step. This is so scary . . .

DAY 14: Apparently, our adrenaline levels were low yesterday—so we went to meet some sharks! While **cage diving**, we went below the surface in a giant metal cage, which is said to protect us from sharp teeth. We sure hoped so!

SNAKE ISLAND

DAY 15: Do you see that **abandoned lighthouse**? About 100 years ago, its last keeper still lived there with his family. One day, the fishermen found them dead. The snakes got to them through an open window ...

DAY 16: Wow, **paragliding** over the sea is an amazing experience! You have a view like a bird, and the fresh wind was amazing! God, Yuna was trying to do somersaults through the air ... It's good she was strapped.

19

BIZARRE PROFESSION

Scientists who study snake venom and make effective antidotes from it, mainly for heart and circulatory diseases, receive permission to enter Snake Island each year. Obtaining the venom is a relatively dangerous process. Experts, commonly called "snake milkers", catch the snake, grasp it professionally, and deftly hold its head, so the snake releases its venom into a prepared glass.

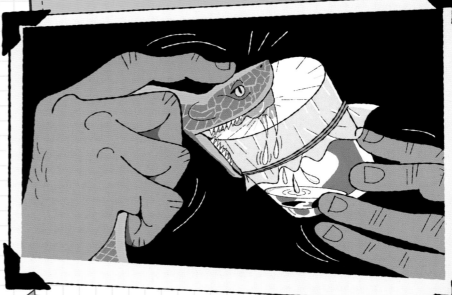

THE SNAKE KNOWS NO MERCY

How could the Lancehead not be dangerous when there is no predator on the island to stand up to it? This is also the reason this barely half-metre-long snake has bred so scarily here. When the sea separated this piece of land from the mainland 11,000 years ago, they multiplied and became **FIVE TIMES** more poisonous than their relatives on the mainland. Without timely help, their venom can kill a person within an hour.

 # BEAST FEAST

Eat some ants!

WRITTEN BY A HUNGRY ANTEATER

Taste giant Amazon ants—the famous Brazilian delicacy! Would you like popular indigenous-style fried insect with sugar or a gourmet version in melted chocolate? Go ahead, the ants are **a great source of protein.** Crunch, crunch, crunch!

PIRATE **TREASURE HUNTERS**

A well-known legend states that snakes were brought here a long time ago by **greedy pirates** to safeguard their hidden treasure. But we were wondering: how in the world did they think they could return for the treasure on an island full of Lanceheads?

Nutrition facts:
HIGHEST IN PROTEIN AND THE FINEST CHOCOLATE!

WHAT TO DO IF YOU GET BITTEN BY A SNAKE

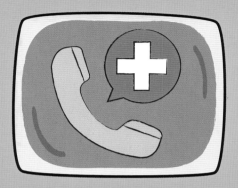

Call an ambulance immediately. Some snake bites do not significantly harm humans, but others can hit organs, cause blindness, and even lead to death.

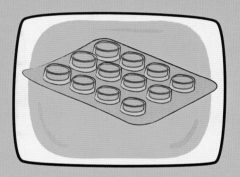

The first aid varies depending on the type of snake that attacked. Do not apply a tourniquet or suck the venom out. **Try to calm the bitten person**, and possibly give them pain medication.

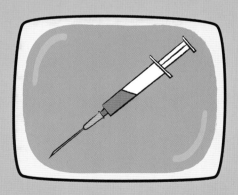

The timely administration of an **anti-venom**, selected according to the specific type of the snake, is a reliable cure. So, don't forget its exact name.

ETNA

Will there be an eruption? And if yes, how strong? Will it put us in danger? These questions plagued us as we landed in Sicily, and the most active volcano in the world greeted us with a massive puff of smoke. This time, however, Etna only displayed harmless but breath-taking colorful fireworks. What an amazing sight! It was as if hell was spilling out to the surface . . .

The lava temperature during the eruption: 1200–2000 °F

DAY 17: This is how you take risks in the name of science! Together with **volcanologists**, we took samples from a fresh lava flow. Even in a protective suit, we felt the heat, with ash particles burning our eyes. The camera glass was completely black from it . . .

DAY 20: Bungee jumping into an active volcano? Why not! The helicopter pilot must, however, fly high enough! The 120-mile speed when falling is a huge adrenaline adventure in itself . . .

DAY 18: Do you see those piles of garbage and full trash cans on every corner? This is the **waste crisis** that southern Italy has been struggling with for a long time. Ugh, a really fat rat just ran under our feet!

DAY 19: Today, we had fun on extinct volcanic craters: **volcano boarding**! Wow, what a ride! Oh no, my favorite trousers! Dang, volcanic gravel . . .

START
2297 ft
64 °F

FINISH
9514 ft
-19 °F

GLASSES AGAINST VOLCANIC DUST

WINTER JACKET

SNOWSHOES

DESTINATION:
~Etna~
(Italy, Sicilia)

9842+ feet high

FROST ON ETNA

Etna is, of course, a mountain that's more than 9842 feet high, which means that its peak is covered with snow for a significant part of the year. Never come here without winter clothes. Trainers are really a stupid idea, says Yuna! While in the lowlands, you can enjoy walking in a T-shirt. Here, however, you will encounter **temperatures below zero**, **strong winds**, and a very slippery terrain. The wind also constantly throws its **volcanic dust** to the air and your eyes.

HOW DO VOLCANOES AFFECT OUR LIVES?

a volcanic eruption =>
release of hot magma*
from the Earth's interior =>
a lava flow => destruction
of the surrounding area
or good source for
a fertilizer!
=========

* a mixture of molten rocks, minerals, and gases waiting in the depths of the planet like a time bomb!

Sicilian street stalls attract you with various kinds of scents. Hmmm, this smells really great! We dared to taste the local specialty, **stigghiola skewers**. It consists of lamb intestines rolled around a leek, which is finally cooked on a grill. Just don't think too much about the production process—it could ruin your appetite. **Yum!**
====

1900   1950   2000   present

At the beginning of the 20th century, Etna was proud of her one huge active crater—but today, she has four! Their formations have been accompanied by massive eruptions, and Etna will continue to change her looks. Many small craters, which are not dangerous yet, are of interest to the tourists, but let's wait, some of them will grow over time . . .

TO BATTLE! **PREPARE YOUR ORANGES!**

The soil surrounding Mount Etna is **extremely fertile**. In addition to grape vines, the locals mainly grow the celebrated **Sicilian blood oranges**, which they export to all of Europe. They also export them to the remote northern Italian town of **Ivrea**, where for centuries, they have been holding a huge orange battle every year! We did not take a trip to Ivrea to watch this madness, so we tried playing catch with our own oranges.

ITALY

IVREA

Visiting the largest cave in the world has long been our dream. It's inconspicuously hidden in the middle of the jungle, and this is the reason only a few daredevils have managed to explore all of its length of 6 miles. Magnificent limestone spaces, in which several houses could be hidden, alternate with slippery narrow passages over the abyss. In the darkness, one can end up trapped forever—now, doesn't that remind you of the movie "The Descent"? *chills* Hang Sơn Đoòng does not share its secrets for free . . .

DAY 21: We started our four-day expedition, which went on in complete darkness. Enlisting our hearing and touching abilities at full capacity, we would be lost without headlamps . . . Wow, look, a stalactite hall!

DAY 22: This time, **we dove deep under the surface of the underground river.** We didn't know what you could see in the camera, because it was like swimming through dark milk . . . A piece of rock—that was close! Hey, white fish!

HANG SƠN ĐOÒNG

DAY 23: We were woken up by warm sunshine. A hallucination, perhaps? No, this is the famous Garden of Eden! A long time ago, the ceiling collapsed and a **unique underground jungle** emerged up here. Can you hear the birds singing?

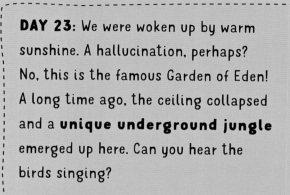

DAY 24: Wait, what? The exit is not until beyond this **Great Wall of Vietnam**?! But it measures around 197 feet—and it's all muddy! Okay, let's find the holes to secure the rope. Otherwise, we'll never get out of here.

UNDERWATER PHOTOGRAPHY

- Waterproof protection for your device is a must. Choose a protection that reliably withstands pressure at greater depths.
- Even in clear water, seemingly invisible dirt floats. The closer you are to the subject, the less the dirt will spoil the shot.
- Use the diving torch at greater depths.
- Try not to use the flash—it only illuminates the dirt in the water.

A GREAT DISCOVERY BY A LITTLE BOY

In the middle of the forest in central Vietnam, a little boy Khanh found the entrance to a cave one day. He already knew some of the local caves, having hidden in them from the rain and the bombs . . . but this was something else. Something huge. It's not easy to find a way in the jungle, and Khanh couldn't locate the place again. Up until 1991, now an adult. Then, 18 years later, he showed the cave to scientists.

OVERNIGHT INSIDE THE CAVE

The first scientific expedition to explore Hang Sơn Đoòng paved the path for later visitors. Who do you think drilled the holes for a rope into the Great Wall of Vietnam? Who widened the hatches in the rock with only tiny slits? We still, of course, had to spend several nights underground, where we could not disturb the natural environment. You can easily destroy an ecosystem that has been here for three million years, for example, by accidentally touching the stalactites—causing irreversible damage.

SNAKE SOUP AND FRIED CRICKETS

I tell you the food at the street stalls in Vietnam smells so tempting! You can dine right in the street. If we had not been so exhausted from the long cave adventure, we would probably have looked at the snake soup with more suspicion, but . . . you just had to stop thinking about the snake skin floating in the soup. In the end, it was very good! Not all of us, however, dared to try the fried crickets. Insects are generally a welcome delicacy in south-east Asia. And why not? They contain a lot of protein. When you overcome your fear, you will enjoy it. And it even crunches!

THE STINKY FRUIT

At the local market, people enticed us to buy durian. It's said to smell terribly, but taste divinely—something like fluffy vanilla ice cream. We were not allowed in taxis and public transport, so we opened the fruit on the spot. It was a gastronomic miracle!

🦢 MODERN SPELEOLOGY ⛏️

1 MAY 2009

In the Phong Nha-Ke Bang National Park in central Vietnam, British speleologists Howard and Deb Limberts confirmed the discovery of the largest known cave in the world, which has been vaguely whispered of among cavers for some time.

The designation "the largest cave in the world" is, of course, controversial in a sense. Mammoth Cave in Kentucky, USA, clearly defeats Hang Son Doong in terms of the length of the discovered corridors; Krubera-Voronja Cave in the Western Caucasus is significantly deeper. Nowhere in the world, however, will you find spaces as vast as the giant passages in the Hang Son Doong cave system. They are sometimes more than 295 feet wide and about 787 feet high . . .

HiMALAYAS

If there's a place perfectly matching the motto "silence before the storm," then it's the village of Dharapani in the foothills of the Himalayas. Just imagine the greenery, little stone houses with windows in blue frames, a roaring wild river in the valley . . . an oasis of peace, right? But we're not here for this idyll. We've planned an expedition at Annapurna tomorrow one of the highest mountains in the world and also the deadliest peak in the Himalayas. The weather is treacherous up there. We'll see how far we get . . .

DAY 25: It was worse than anything we could've imagined! After a few days' hike, there were only **steep barren slopes, rocks, and snow**. More and more snow. It was slippery, and the wind was getting stronger . . . Are we even able to go a little further?

DAY 26: Oliver has **acute mountain sickness**. We had to return to the base camp. My goodness, this was bad. Luck was not on our side. We gave up on the attempt to climb to the peak this time . . .

DAY 27: Thank goodness, Oliver got better. So, we tried **hang gliding**—flying in a hang glider without an engine. Above us, only wings. Below us, meadows, houses, and mountains. The idyll was back!

DAY 28: Rafting on a raging river was no fun. We just narrowly avoided sharp stones at our speed . . . Uh-oh, watch out, rapids! Oh dear, no! I was soaking wet! Um, could they hear me? I think the white water destroyed the microphone . . .

IN THE **BASE CAMP**

When Oliver felt sick and couldn't breathe, we were grateful that we weren't far from the **base camp**—the lodge en route to the summit. The base camp is not only a springboard for climbing Annapurna itself, it's also a perfect haven for those who don't want to climb further but want to merely admire it from afar.

Did you know that a Sherpa named Tenzing Norgay was the first, along with Edmund Hillary from New Zealand, to climb Mt. Everest?

SERENITY IN THE FOOTHILLS

People from all over the world travel to the **Himalayas these days**—some of them far from skilled climbers. You don't have to attempt 8000 peaks to enjoy yourself here: spend days wandering through the mountain forests, climbing the hills at a slower pace and enjoying the breathtaking views of the mountains. The local villagers are renowned for their hospitality as they offer you a cheap place to sleep. The dangerous zones start much, much higher, while down here, it's more of a paradise for those seeking tranquility and even themselves . . .

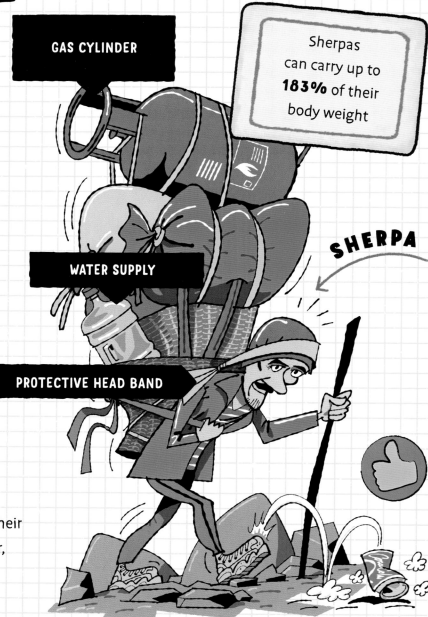

GAS CYLINDER

Sherpas can carry up to **183%** of their body weight

WATER SUPPLY

SHERPA

PROTECTIVE HEAD BAND

The Sherpas, local porters and guides of climbing and hiking expeditions, are just unreal. They carry a load you probably couldn't even pick up off the ground! They come from the local villages, which means they know the Himalayas like the back of their hands, can predict weather changes, and are used to the alpine air, so they don't suffer from the **lack of oxygen** at the top.

ACUTE **MOUNTAIN SICKNESS**

Acute mountain sickness easily affects anyone who climbs to alpine altitudes too fast. There, the atmospheric pressure is low and the human body has to gradually acclimatize. The ideal rate of ascent is only around 1300 feet per day. If you experience dizziness, weakness, poor sleep, slow breathing, sickness in your stomach, immediately descend to a lower altitude. People who underestimate this face the risk of losing consciousness and even their life.

FIERY CURRY AND **BUTTER TEA**

We were really looking forward to the first meal after our infamous descent from the mountains. The villagers prepared meat curry for us, the spiciness of which made us burst into tears! We tried to cool down the infernal burning in our throats with rice followed by the traditional drink of butter tea. Tibetans drink the butter tea by the bucket load. They can even handle 60 cups a day. In the mountains, it provides energy and protects the lips against frostbite.

So far, we have traveled through many kinds of wilderness, but millions of children experience everyday adventures in the middle of modern cities with state-of-the-art buildings thriving in an inhospitable desert. Glass skyscrapers, luxurious parks and gardens, and historic houses crouching in the shade of new buildings are also places where you can meet extremes. Come join us in the Arabian Peninsula! We'll find out soon whether or not the desert is lifeless . . .

DAY 32: Like hundreds of years ago, **Bedouins** roam the inhospitable desert. The sand and arid mountains are their home. Well, not everyone has a preference for a comfortable life among skyscrapers . . .

DAY 31: Just outside the city borders, we tried **sandboarding**. It's like snowboarding, but without snow—you ride sand dunes. Despite the scorching heat, we had a great time!

ARABIAN PENINSULA

DAY 29: During **parkour**—overcoming walls, railings, stairs, terraces, and other obstacles deftly, without touching the ground—you get a new perspective on the city jungle.

DAY 30: Is this a haunted house? Shush! Strange things have been happening here for some time. Even **paranormal investigators** can't explain them... Aaaah, what was that? Yuna? We were outta there.

HEAT STROKE AND HEAT ILLNESS, TWO DANGEROUS ENEMIES

In direct sunlight → **heat stroke**
In the heat → **heat illness**

What are the symptoms?
- Headache
- Malaise and fatigue
- Fever and confusion
- Nausea and vomiting
- Hot skin (**heat stroke**) or dry skin without sweating (**heat illness**)
- Accelerated breathing and rapid palpitations (**heat illness**)
- Spasm (**heat illness**)
- Shock and unconsciousness (**heat illness**)

What can I do?
- Look for a cool place in the shade.
- Take a cold shower (**heat illness**) or apply a cold compress to cool down your head (**heat stroke**).
- In case of more serious problems, lie down and call an ambulance.

If you need to go outside in hot weather:
- Don't forget to drink enough water (preferably mineral).
- Protect your head and skin well.
- Stay in the shade.

TEMPERATURES DURING THE YEAR

=> January 55–68 °F

=> April 86–104 °F

=> July 113–122 °F

=> October 77–86 °F

TERRIBLE HEAT

During the day, temperatures in the cities of the Arabian Peninsula climb to incredible **122 degrees Fahrenheit**. Crazy, right? In such heat, the human body overheats rapidly, and one can even die. It's like spending the whole day in a tropical greenhouse!

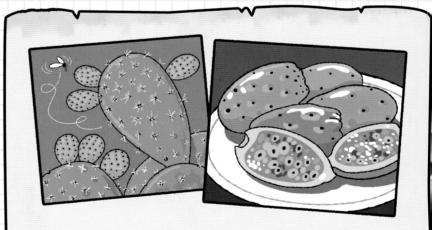

HMMM, WHAT A DELICIOUS ... CACTUS

Have you ever eaten a cactus? We came across orange, yellow, and red prickly fruits of prickly pear, a cactus native to Mexico, at the local market, where the seller offered us a piece to taste. Of course, the fruits are processed only after the thorns are removed—then, they are an incredibly sweet and healthy delicacy!

CAN'T SEE ANYTHING BECAUSE OF THE SAND . . .

A sandstorm caught us at the end of our stay but lasted three whole days. The desert sand shrouded the city like a huge hungry dragon, blocked the sun, and suddenly spread everywhere—**EVERYWHERE**! We could not see more than six feet ahead of us, and life in the city practically came to a stop. There is nothing to prevent the winds that blow through the desert from striking human settlements, no matter how super modern, with full force.

AN ACCIDENT IN THE LABORATORY!

During one parkour session, we noticed ambulances, fire trucks, and police patrols gathering near a wide avenue. Soon, the pavement was filled with uniformed paramedics resembling astronauts. Apparently, there was an explosion in a local university laboratory. And because the emergency service could not tell yet if toxic chemicals had escaped, they had to proceed as if they had. And they say scientific work is boring . . .

AMERICAN MIDWEST

Originally, we were only supposed to drive through the American Midwest. But sometimes, plans just don't work out, and a tornado pulled the brakes on our plans. We immediately went to the affected area to offer help, but we had no idea that the weather would decide to test the will and perseverance of the locals again. So now, we're standing in the middle of a town hit by flash floods and trying to help as much as we can. And to make matters worse, another tornado is rushing toward the district!

DAY 33: Firefighters rescuing people and animals from flooded houses on boats avoid floating cars and furniture in the muddy water. For those who suddenly lost every-thing, we offered hot tea at least.

DAY 36: How many hands do you need to save all the **animals from the flooded zoo**? The more the better, of course! Ouch, the parrot pecked my ear, help!

DAY 34: A **measuring vehicle** is a complicated mobile device that monitors the formation and movement of a tornado. Silence and no wind are the warning signs. And we don't feel good about the strange green sky either . . .

DAY 35: This footage was taken for us by the **"tornado hunters"**. They love risk-taking and observe tornadoes up close. Fools! One tiny mistake, and there's no escape . . .

WHEN A STORM STRIKES

Predicting a tornado is not easy, although meteorologists are more successful today than ever before. It usually occurs during a **supercell***. Due to the varying hot and cold air, the storm cloud transforms into a vertical funnel. It rotates faster and faster until it touches the ground. By that time, it gathers unimaginable force, destroying whatever comes in its way. It is often accompanied by flash floods, which people can't prepare for beforehand.

WHAT'S WORSE THAN A TORNADO?

TWO TORNADOES

Once every 10 to 15 years, the weather will amaze even experienced scientists: during a storm, two tornadoes will form next to each other **from just one supercell**. So, they are like devilish twins. Have you ever wondered what our ancestors imagined tornadoes to be? Wild devils raging over the landscape.

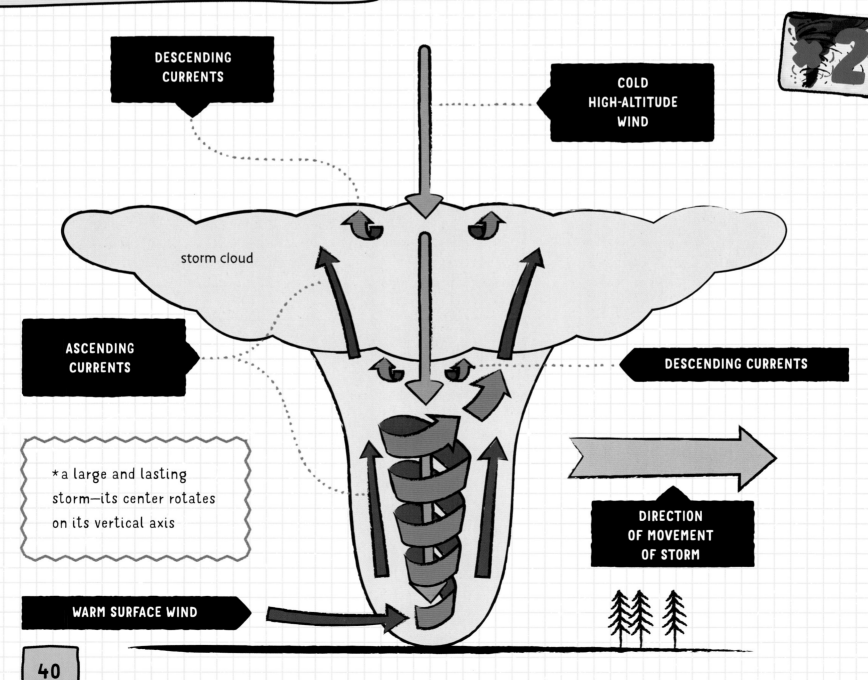

DESCENDING CURRENTS

COLD HIGH-ALTITUDE WIND

storm cloud

ASCENDING CURRENTS

DESCENDING CURRENTS

*a large and lasting storm—its center rotates on its vertical axis

DIRECTION OF MOVEMENT OF STORM

WARM SURFACE WIND

OYSTERS ARE NOT ALWAYS OYSTERS

Our last adventure was much more unpleasant than we'd planned. We were relieved when the water receded, the wind calmed down, and we were finally able to go to the airport. But we returned much later on a food adventure. The locals we'd gotten to know warmly invited us to a renowed and restored restaurant for some excellent Midwestern **"mountain oysters"**. But wait, um . . . what . . . these don't look like oysters! Excuse me, what are we eating? Jeez! So mountain oysters aren't oysters at all—they're, uh, bull's testicles!

LIVE **BROADCASTING**

Today, it is no longer necessary to have a transmission car for live broadcasts. A single mobile phone and microphone is enough! But always research as much as possible beforehand. If you plan to record an authentic interview, you should stick to pre-arranged questions—if something distracts you, you will be able to be spontaneous.

USE a mobile set for live streaming

camcorder   camera

WHEN A **TORNADO IS APPROACHING**

• If you're inside, hide in the basement and cover yourself with mattresses or blankets. If there is no basement in the house, a hall, bathroom, or other room without windows on the ground floor will do the job. Crouch as low as you can, facing the floor, and cover your head with your hands.

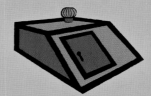 

Be safe in a storm shelter!

• Avoid windows, elevators, large indoor spaces (such as gyms), and caravans.

• If there's no possibility of escaping into the building, lie on the ground as far away from cars and trees as possible. Never hide under a bridge, because the wind under it will be stronger.

AND WHAT NEXT . . .

We are spending most of our time in the editing room. We go through the materials shot by shot on the computer monitors. We cut, move, and sometimes, keep the original sound. In other parts, we come up with new commentary or suitable background music. It's a complete science—which is why our Daniel enjoys it the most.

"I've kept all the tickets and leaflets that passed through my hands during the expedition. Now, we can take pictures of the most interesting ones and add them to our show."

Interviews
→ Inuit fisherman
→ Himalayan Sherpa
→ Soldier from Snake Island
SUBTITLES OR DUBBING?

"In the editing room, we are now adding an audio background to some of our shots of the landscape—a reading from our travel journal."

If you find yourself intrigued and want to start shooting your own show—yay! Now, you also know a little about how it works. We're happy for you! Maybe, we'll meet on another adventure!

No comment
=> woodland fire in Canada
=> night sky over Atacama
=> erupting Etna at night
=> incoming tornado (recorded by the tornado hunters)

When shooting a documentary, it's exhausting to watch similar shots over and over again. Switch between spoken commentary and interviews with interesting people, and if you have managed to shoot something truly extraordinary, don't be afraid to include such shots in your show just like that, without any comment. The more varied your show is, the better is the viewing experience.

TABLE OF CONTENTS

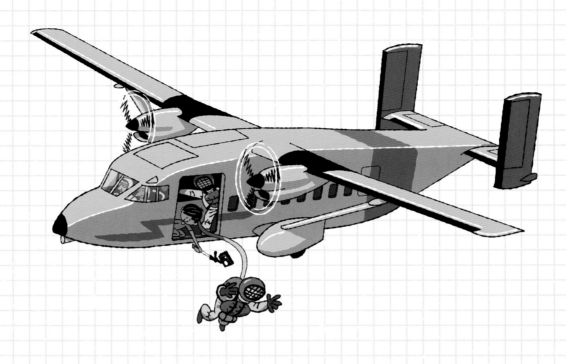

© B4U Publishing for Albatros,
an imprint of Albatros Media Group, 2022
5. května 1746/22, Prague 4, Czech Republic

Written by Helena Haraštová
Illustrated by Lukáš Fibrich
Infographic illustrations by Martin Urbánek
Translated by David Livingstone

Printed in China by Leo Paper Group

ISBN: 978-80-00-06601-1